# BECOMING A
# NEW YORK STATE

**Louis Larson**
*State University of New York at Cortland*

**Joy Mosher**
*State University of New York at Cortland*

THOMSON
WADSWORTH

Australia • Canada • Mexico • Singapore
Spain • United Kingdom • United States

For more information about our products, contact us at:
**Thomson Learning Academic Resource Center**
**1-800-423-0563**

**For permission to use material from this text, contact us by:**
**Phone: 1-800-730-2214**
**Fax: 1-800-731-2215**
**Web:** http://www.thomsonrights.com

**Asia**
Thomson Learning
5 Shenton Way #01-01
UIC Building
Singapore 068808

**Australia/ New Zeland**
Nelson Thomson Learning
102 Dodds Street
South Street
Southbank, Victoria 3006
Australia

**Canada**
Nelson
1120 Birchmount Road
Toronto, Ontario M1K 5G4
Canada

**Europe/Middle East**
**South Africa**
Thomson Learning
High Holborn House
50/51 Bedford Row
London WC1R 4LR
United Kingdom

**Latin America**
Thomson Learning
Seneca, 53
Colonia Polanco
11560 Mexico D.F.
Mexico

**Spain/ Portugal**
Paraninfo
Calle/Magallanes, 25
28015 Madrid, Spain

# Table of Contents

# Introduction

Congratulations on your commitment to a noble profession. The information in this supplement will guide you through the process of becoming a teacher in the State of New York. Significant changes have been made in New York State Standards for Education and requirements and policies regarding certification, with the goal of improving the educational experiences of children. February 2004 is the effective date of new regulations for teacher certification in New York State.

The process of becoming a teacher in New York State has become more rigorous, as it should. Professionalism is the hallmark of excellence. Democracies need citizens who have a wide range of knowledge, ability to think critically and who have a commitment to social justice. Educational institutions provide the environment and teachers provide the means to achieve this goal.

Preparing for a career in education should begin *now*. The college program, testing and certification requirements are only part of the picture. Your volunteer and course-related experiences in the community and with children and educators contribute significantly to your professionalism. Career preparation extends throughout your education as you develop the knowledge, skills and experiences that make you a qualified and desirable candidate. We recommend the following sequence of activities, which will be discussed further in the chapters of this supplement.

# Sequence of Activities

## Upon Entering the Teacher Preparation Program

- Set and maintain goals for the personal, academic and professional reputation required for the degree and reviewed by prospective employers.

- Develop experiences in the community and with children that relate to your unique goals and skills.

- Begin collecting artifacts that demonstrate your particular knowledge and experiences.

- Take time for critical reflection about the fit of the career with your unique identity and goals.

## Before the Student Teaching Experience

- Complete the New York State workshops and tests required for certification.

- Establish a credentials file.

## During the Student Teaching Experience

- Review and complete the credentials file.

- Develop the job-application portfolio.

## During the Final Semester

- Review/confirm completion of all requirements.

- Review the credentials file.

- Make a decision about a job search or graduate school.

- Finalize the portfolio, resume and application letters.

# About the Authors

Louis Larson is Assistant Director of Career Services at the State University of New York, Cortland College. He works with undergraduate and graduate students in all SUNY Cortland departments. In a given year, Louis provides workshops and individual counseling to thousands of pre-service candidates for positions in the field of education.

Joy Mosher is Associate Professor of Education at the State University of New York, Cortland College. Joy teaches courses in classroom discipline and early childhood literacy across the curriculum. She has a particular interest in migrant education.

We would like to thank Virginia Levine, Ph.D., Associate Dean of Teacher Certification and Accreditation at SUNY Cortland for her cheerful responsiveness, undivided attention and masterful knowledge of complex information. We are indebted to the Career Services Staff at SUNY Cortland for their professional expertise and their attention to detail in gathering certification and job search information.

# Chapter 1
# Perspectives on Teaching

*Why do I want to be a teacher?*

*How do I find the right school for me, as a teacher?*

*What special skills or knowledge can I offer to my school and students?*

In any endeavor, it is important to find the right work environment. Developing a career in teaching requires more than thinking about the job. Take time for careful reflection about your goals, values and individual needs. Course content and practical experiences provide the raw material for that deliberation. If you are to be an excellent teacher, and if teaching is to be a rewarding and fulfilling career, you must know yourself, in order to know what you want and what you have to offer.

When it comes to teaching, the fit is especially important because of the significant influence teachers have upon students. That influence is not merely academic, but personal and moral as well. Teachers educate all the other professions, from kindergarten through graduate school. The just and responsive citizenry of a democracy is built upon the educational experiences of children; teachers play a pivotal role in the education of the citizens of a society. Throughout your experiences with children in formal and informal settings, the following considerations will help you prepare to find the right job. Each experience also offers the chance to collect artifacts for use as you assemble a portfolio that speaks to who you are as a person and a teacher.

**Finding the Best Environment**

*Do I enjoy working with the children, in both their successes and challenges?*

*Are the goals and attitudes toward children of the educators in this school consistent with my own goals and attitudes?*

*Are administrators and teachers effective, positive models and mentors to support my own development?*

*Can I do my best work in this environment?*

It is important to gain experience with a variety of children in a variety of settings. While all children have developmental and academic needs, many factors influence how those needs are expressed and how they should be addressed. Rural, suburban and urban settings may pose very different obstacles and rewards. Particular economic or social conditions may require specialized skills or significant dedication on the part of the teacher. A good match between the challenges and joys of a particular position and your own values and skills can make teaching a truly rewarding experience.

It is important to think of yourself in relationship to the school community and culture. Consider the kind of association you have with teachers and administrators. Examine the ways peers and administrators contribute to your growth, and the ways you can contribute to theirs. Each teacher should be an integral part of the whole of the school.

Knowing the community and the nature of community support for the schools is important. Find out about travel time to the

2

school, the cost of living and community resources. Imagine living in the community for a number of years and sending your own children to the schools. Think of yourself as an important member of that community.

## The Right Teacher for the Right Job

*What makes me the best candidate for this particular position?*

*What knowledge of particular topics or issues do I have?*

*What skills have I developed for sharing that knowledge?*

District administrators often say that there are many bright, qualified candidates for every position, but the administrators seek teachers to fit well in their particular school environment. Administrators want to know what unique knowledge and skills teacher candidates offer. Is the candidate skilled in the use of conflict resolution strategies? Is the candidate knowledgeable about integrated curriculum or cooperative approaches to learning? Can the candidate direct the school play or conduct a lunch time activity period?

Just as you must assess the fit of the school and community with your own needs, you should think about how prospective employers view your background. Completion of your degree and certification requirements qualifies you as a candidate, but that is merely the beginning. What factors make you the best candidate, among many qualified competitors? As you begin your teacher preparation program, consider ways to develop your own unique interest areas and expertise.

Your college experiences offer the chance for extended or specialized experiences with children. Here are some possibilities:

- Volunteer work tutoring or mentoring a child

- Volunteer work with groups of children with special needs.

- Work in an after-school or summer program or camp.

- Experience in sports, music, drama, clubs etc., both as a participant and an organizer of events for children

In the process of academic course work, you may become interested in a particular topic or issue. Lectures and workshops may stimulate an interest. You may attend a conference related to your profession or a particular topic or issue. As you find and develop these special interest areas, you will have opportunities to share that knowledge with others. Here are some examples of topics and ways to share knowledge:

- Class or across-class presentations on special topics or issues directly related to children, e.g. literacy, English as a Second Language, Children and Grief, The Experiences of Migrant Students or Gifted Students, or Children with Different Kinds of Families.

- Presentations or workshops on those topics on campus, in the community or at conferences.

- Service work with related groups on campus and in the community.

## Assembling a Portfolio

As you work in a variety of settings, gather artifacts to help you reflect upon your experiences and organize them into a coherent account. This portfolio helps document your accomplishments and helps you assess your interests and strengths. Here are some possibilities:

- Essays or class projects pertinent to your interests.

- Photographs of yourself in your professional role, bulletin boards, centers, events that you created, and so on.

- Journals and other reflective pieces.

- A copy of lesson plans and unit plans you developed.

- Teacher and supervisor feedback on your performance.

- Examples of student work.

- Messages or comments written to you by students, parents, teachers and administrators.

The portfolio is not a static collection or a mere accumulation of material. It is a dynamic collection of artifacts. Careful reflection discloses themes and interests. The portfolio is a resource as you put together an application for employment or a graduate-school interview.

## Frequently Asked Questions

**How can I determine the area of teaching best suited to my interests and abilities? How do I know teaching is the right career for me?**

Long before completing the education program, you should work with children of various ages in a variety of settings. Volunteer in a variety of classrooms and in other organizations that serve children. Talk with teachers in different areas. Think carefully about what you see and hear and feel. Careful consideration of these experiences builds the conviction that you have chosen the right career, or raises questions about your goals.

**Are my work experiences in businesses, factories, restaurants, etc. relevant to a teaching career?**

Yes. Many skills for accomplishing goals and working effectively with others are developed. Sometimes, particular school districts appreciate the match between a candidate's experiences and the community.

**What if I prepare to be a teacher, then later decide I would like to pursue another career?**

The skills and knowledge developed in preparation for teaching apply in a variety of careers. Public speaking, research and writing are valuable attributes in any profession. The excellent communication, leadership, organizational, time-management and *people* skills, and the attention to detail and creativity that is common in good teachers will make you a valuable candidate for many career positions.

# Chapter 2
# The New York State Teacher

*What teaching opportunities are available in New York State?*

*What standards are established for students in New York State and what tests are administered?*

*What teacher responsibilities are related to New York State Standards for Learning and standardized tests?*

*What support is available to help teachers meet New York State Standards for Learning and New York State Standards for Teachers?*

*How are teachers evaluated in New York State?*

*How do college programs prepare teachers to meet the needs of students in New York State?*

There are many career choices for teachers in New York State. In addition to work in the classroom at all grade levels, educators serve in a variety of other positions, for example as bilingual educators, reading specialists, special education teachers, and teachers of English as a second language (ESL). College Career Centers and academic departments can provide further information regarding a particular field of teaching. Teacher salaries are based on degree status, certification level, and years of service. Other factors, such as incentives or the district location also affect teacher salaries.

In 1996, New York State began a dramatic and far-reaching reform of elementary, middle and secondary education. The

New York State Board of Regents established the Professional Standards and Practices Board, a group of recognized, outstanding educators and public representatives which advises the Regents and Commissioner on critical issues relating to the quality of teaching and teacher education in New York State. The State proposed professional development and teacher certification requirements, due to take effect in February 2004. The State adopted clear, rigorous standards for teachers and initiated steps to recruit and retain the best teachers in areas where they are most needed. The State legislation calls for school districts to develop a high level of competence in teachers through effective induction for new teachers and professional development for all teachers.

New York State faces a shortage of qualified teachers, particularly minority teachers and teachers in some subject areas and geographic locations. The State has taken a variety of steps to increase teacher availability and recruitment, including financial, educational and workplace incentives.

## The New York State Standards for Learning

Concerns across the nation about student achievement and preparation for effective participation in society resulted in close scrutiny of schools and student progress. Prompted by these concerns, New York State strengthened expectations and requirements for student content knowledge and performance. The Board of Regents approved learning standards, which establish a baseline of what all people should know, understand and be able to do as a result of their education.

The New York State Learning Standards include all areas of the curriculum and establish required knowledge and skills for students in all grades. Teachers prepare learning experiences within these requirements to help students meet the standards and prepare for State tests, which assess that achievement.

Teachers plan lessons with reference to the New York State Standards for Learning. Teachers must be prepared to explain to parents and community members how these activities help children meet standards and develop important knowledge and skills. Similarly, teacher assessment of lessons and student performance is based upon the New York State Standards for Learning.

### Grade-level Tests

To assess student achievement and school support of that achievement, the New York State Board of Regents established testing in English Language Arts and Mathematics for all elementary students in Grade 4 and all middle school students in Grade 8. The tests assess not only basic skills, but applied knowledge. Individual scores are recorded in the student's cumulative file; they provide a profile of a student's strengths and weaknesses in a variety of skill areas. Student performance scores are aggregated and become part of documentation of school performance.

### Regents Examinations

New York State requires Regents Examinations for all students in the following curricular areas: Global Studies, U.S. History; Mathematics; English; Science (several subject area examinations may be taken). The tests are administered in 10th, 11th and 12th grades, depending on the subject. This is one means by which the Board of Regents assesses and assures the consistent quality of subject mastery in New York State schools. All students who graduate from a high school in the State of New York will receive either a *Regents Diploma* or a *Regents Diploma with Distinction*. The primary difference between the two diplomas is the number of credits taken and coursework and a proficiency test in a foreign language. A passing grade on the Regents Examinations is required to obtain a Regents diploma from the school district/state. Scores on Regents examinations become part of a student's permanent record, noted in the student's cumulative file and high school transcript.

## District Assessment of Student Performance

The standardized tests administered to students provide important information to local districts about student and teacher performance. Teachers, grade level teams and administrators in local schools and districts assess that data within the context of the community, in order to better meet the learning needs of students. Information about student performance is disseminated through the School Report Card and other documents, available from the office of the local school board or the web site of the New York State Education Department. Local media report aggregated achievement scores, comparing local districts. Test data are also used to identify schools that need to improve the student performance.

## State and Public Assessment of School Performance

In compliance with the federal *No Child Left Behind* act, New York State identifies public districts and schools in need of improvement. The New York State Education Department collects and disseminates information related to student achievement, by district and school. Each school in New York State receives a School Report Card, which lists student achievement in reading, mathematics and other subjects. It also lists the number of teachers rated *unsatisfactory* during the preceding school year, the number of Teacher Improvement Plans which were not completed successfully, and the number of proceedings initiated to terminate employment because of unsatisfactory completion of the Teacher Improvement Plan. A school with a record of poor student achievement is identified as a *School Under Registration Review*. If significant improvement has not occurred after a specified period of time, the State may choose to close down the school or take other steps to address the problem.

### The New York State Teacher Standards

New York State established Teacher Standards, which clearly identify the required knowledge and skills for teachers, in order to meet the learning needs of students. The New York State Teacher Standards are congruent with the teaching standards established by national professional education organizations. These teaching standards shape teacher education programs, certification examinations and other requirements, and teacher performance requirements in New York State.

Certified teachers in New York State implement lessons and assess student progress with reference to a complex and well developed set of curricular standards and tests for all students. Standardized tests are administered to all students in elementary school, middle school and high school. Teachers work with other teachers in their districts to assess student progress and the implications for their own practice. At every

11

grade level, teachers must prepare and implement lessons with reference to expectations for students in New York State.

## The New York State Code of Ethics for Teachers

The New York State Board of Regents, as part of its teaching reform initiatives called for the State Professional Standards and Practices Board for Teaching to develop a Code of Ethics for Teachers. Any individual for whom a certificate is required for service will be held accountable to this Code of Ethics. For further information, see Chapter 9 *Resources*.

## Support and Assessment of Teacher Performance

The State Board of Regents requires school districts in New York State to regularly provide induction support to new teachers and professional development activities for all teachers in the district. The professional development experiences must be linked to the learning needs of students, as identified in the district School Report Card and State initiatives, standards and assessments. All teachers receiving a professional certificate after September, 2000 are required to successfully complete at least 175 hours of professional development every five years. Teachers must complete professional development as a condition of maintaining their certificates in good standing.

## Mentoring

New York State's proposed professional development and teacher certification requirements include the establishment of teacher mentoring programs. The requirements for Professional Certification include one year of mentored teaching. School districts are to provide this mentoring, as part of the process of induction for new teachers. Draft Guidelines for Implementing District Based Teacher Mentoring Programs and other informative documents on mentoring are available at the Web site. See Chapter 9: *Resources* for further information.

## National Board Certification

The New York State Regents support a Master Teacher Program. Outstanding teachers with Permanent or Professional Certification may, with the support of the school board, apply to the Commissioner for grants to support application for advanced certification from the National Board for Professional Teaching Standards (NBPTS). Teachers who receive NBPTS certification with New York State support agree to provide peer assistance, and will be considered for membership on the New York State Professional Standards and Practices Board.

## Teacher Evaluation

While it is understood that student scores on grade-level tests reflect those students' individual skills and previous educational experiences, it is also understood that effective teachers must meet the learning needs of students and prepare the great majority to perform well.

School administrators must regularly assess the performance of teachers; all teachers in a district receive annual performance reviews. Typically, teachers are reviewed for tenure at the end of the third year of teaching in a school district. Tenure grants permanent status in the district. Certain offenses, for example the commission of a felony, violation of the Teacher Code of

Ethics or insubordination warrant the removal of a tenured teacher from a position. Teachers may also lose a school or district position in the event of a necessary reduction in workforce, due to declining enrollment.

The school district must provide assistance to teachers who perform poorly, in order to help them improve their performance. This process is documented in a Teacher Improvement Plan. If the Teacher Improvement Plan is not completed successfully, the administrators may take steps to remove the teacher from the classroom.

## Teacher Education Programs Prepare for Excellence

Educators in New York State understand that teacher excellence and performance serve in the best interests of students as they master important learning and skills. Preparation for that responsibility begins in the teacher education program. A foundation of liberal learning helps teachers develop a love of learning in children. Pedagogy coursework is the starting point for teaching, but many other experiences contribute to teacher excellence. Student teaching and other work in schools helps preservice teachers learn more about New York State standards and tests, and learn more about the ways schools and teachers meet the needs of children and the requirements of the State.

New York State Teacher Standards require effective teacher skills for working with peers and community agencies. Public school administrators emphasize the importance of collegial skills. As one administrator said, the days when teachers could shut the classroom door and function autonomously are gone forever. Teachers collaborate with others to assess their own students' performance and school-wide performance in order to support the achievement and well being of all the children.

During the teacher education program, you have the opportunity to work collegially in professional organizations, clubs and volunteer activities. Many courses require cooperative projects. Such experiences help you learn about using cooperative approaches in teaching; they also help you learn to work effectively with peers.

Our society often celebrates individualism and competition. It may seem more "efficient" or "easy" to do a task alone. While this may seem to be an effective strategy, it bypasses important learning and skill development. The goal is not personal and the outcome extends beyond the product itself. Consequently, it is important to take advantage of opportunities to work with others, and to remember that such efforts develop your professional skill as a teacher and member of a school staff.

Sound background knowledge in the liberal arts, a thorough understanding of planning and implementing curriculum and effective skills for work with children and adults are essential elements excellent teaching. Careful attention to these areas will help you become the kind of teacher New York State needs and requires.

## Frequently Asked Questions

### How can I master the needed knowledge of standards and curriculum when I am a new teacher?

New York State school districts are committed to strong teacher performance and, on the basis of proposed legislation will provide induction support for new teachers. Candidates for the Professional Degree are required to have one year of mentored teaching, in addition to other years of service. In some areas, Teacher Centers serve this function. Colleges and universities are also potential resources as partners with school districts, providing support to graduates as they step into teaching.

### What incentives are offered for teaching in New York State?

New York State has established financial, educational and workplace incentives to recruit minority teachers and teachers for certain high-need areas. See Chapter 9 *Resources* for further information.

### What teacher salaries are typical in New York State?

Teacher salaries in New York State vary significantly, by geographic area. There is no State mandate for teacher salaries: each school district has its own salary schedule. In 2002, the average starting teacher salary in Long Island and Westchester was in the high $30,000 to low $40,000 range. The average starting teacher salary in 2002, in central and western New York was between $34,000 and $37,000. Salary is based on degrees, certification level and years of service.

# Chapter 3
# The College Academic Career

*How is my coursework and academic reputation important to my career?*

*Who will mentor me?*

*When should I begin professional career preparation?*

As you begin a program of required courses it is important to keep an eye on the big picture. Your reputation as a teacher/scholar and a person is already developing. The minimum grade point average for your program and for review by prospective employers, is only the first step.

## Coursework

Take time to reflect upon the relevance of your courses to your chosen career. Theoretical background knowledge forms the context of your professional expertise. This is a good time for critical reflection on how your college program fits your personal and professional goals. As you design the major, the minor and other coursework, pay attention to the developing intellectual focus and interests. Be on the lookout for subject and practical areas that attract you. In the process of course-required research, a topic or an issue may intrigue you. Think of ways you can further develop that area.

Seek volunteer experiences to inform and extend the developing theoretical background. Ideally, a theme will emerge as the program nears completion. This theme speaks to your individual values and interests, and attests to your unique qualifications as a professional. You may find that this interest area becomes a strong point in your portfolio and your desirability as a job candidate. You may also find that this area becomes the research focus of your graduate program.

## Academic Excellence

It is important to do your best and strive to achieve honors that are within your reach; much can be done to develop your reputation in these areas. Set high academic goals, and avail yourself of support to help you achieve them. Most instructors are happy to discuss course content and your performance. Make the most of office hours, extra seminars, academic skill support programs and other opportunities to enhance your learning and skills. These activities do not merely serve to address difficulties; wise students take advantage of the opportunity to optimize their performance.

Peer study and review groups enhance your mastery of material and develop your leadership and collegial skills. While not every student will graduate *magna cum laude*, every student can build a sterling reputation and enhance academic performance collegial skills.

## Character

As you work, study and engage in social activities in college, your reputation is already developing. It is good to be known: take care with what people know of you. It is essential to maintain an impeccable personal and academic reputation. Judicial reviews within the college and legal charges in the community can hinder recommendation for a position, or prevent you from being awarded certification or hired. The office of the Commissioner of Education in New York State conducts fingerprint supported criminal history background checks for all school personnel, including applicants for certification. Conversely, a reputation for integrity and excellence can lead to mentoring, awards, recommendations and employment in desirable positions.

## Mentors

Wherever you go, you will encounter skilled and knowledgeable people. Many will be willing to share their wisdom and expertise, and to encourage and guide you. Seek them out and find time to talk with them.

Mentors within the college may come from your department, other academic areas, organizations, support services, etc. Many of them were mentored when they were in college and were beginning their careers. They are serious about their responsibility to extend that same mentoring to others. These mentors can make a significant contribution to your job search and your development as a new professional.

You will find other mentors in your employment and volunteer placements. Each mentor has different background knowledge and expertise that can enhance your understanding and your performance. Each is a valuable resource.

### Active Participation in the Mentoring Relationship

Your role in the relationship with mentors is not a passive one. The more familiar you are with your own goals and needs, the more deliberate you can be about developing valuable contacts and experiences. Be proactive as you build relationships.

Become acquainted with a wide variety of individuals. Think carefully about what you would like to know, and what you need to know. Who have you worked with that is a good resource?

As you work with mentors, consider the reputation you are developing. Does the character and professionality you demonstrate reward the investment of their time and energy? There are many ways that these people can provide valuable support: among them, are advice, guidance, contacts and possible references for employment.

## Documenting Your Experiences

It is important to begin collecting artifacts, which demonstrate your unique experiences and strengths. Be sure to collect business cards, school publications, business prospectuses, photographs, letters, and other materials that document your interests, activities and learning. These will serve as valuable resources for your portfolio.

## Workshops and Tests

Before student teaching it is advisable to complete tests required by the college and New York State. Several tests and workshops are required for certification; some college programs include them as graduation requirements. New York State mandates workshops in Child Abuse Recognition and Reporting (CARR) and Safe Schools Against Violence Education (SAVE). Three standardized tests are required for Initial Certification: the Liberal Arts and Science Test (LAST), the Assessment of Teaching Skills-Written (ATS-W) and the Content Specialty Test (CST). Some programs currently only require the LAST and ATS-W for graduation, and some certification areas do not require the CST until application for Professional Certification. Check with the New York State Education Department for specific information. Further information on the tests is provided in Chapter 5: *Certification*.

It is advisable to complete the workshops and the LAST and the ATS-W before student teaching. The CST is also required for initial certification; it may be advisable to take it during the college program, while the information is still fresh in your mind.

### Establishing the Credential File

It is advisable to establish a credential file after completing one or two semesters in the education program, when you have identified your field of study and have developed some broad career goals. The credential file contains letters of recommendation, which will be sent by the Credential Office to a designated school and/or district.

A cover letter and resume must accompany each application for a teaching position. Cover letters and resumes should be developed early in your academic career, typically during your second year of coursework, before student teaching. This early start is advantageous for a variety of reasons. Applications for scholarships, awards, substitute teaching, internships, etc. often require a resume. Early resume preparation helps you prepare for graduation and the job search.

Before student teaching, the resume and cover letter should be fairly intact. Thus during the last semester of coursework, as the candidate approaches graduation and makes a decision about a job search or application to graduate school, the file is ready. When you are ready to begin applying, "activate" the credentials file. Further information on the credential file and the job search is provided in Chapter Six: *The Marketing Plan*.

## Frequently Asked Questions

**I was involved in a Judicial Review early in my college career. Will this one experience be noted somewhere for a prospective employer to see?**

Typically, the first offense does not appear on a candidate's transcript. Check your college policy for further details.

**I have little time for clubs. Will this affect my job search?**

Participation in clubs and organizations is valuable experience. Membership in one carefully selected organization, e.g. an honor society might be a helpful solution to your problem.

**Does my coursework reflect current educational theory and trends?**

All applicants for certification must graduate from a State approved teacher education program. These programs must be nationally certified; the program content and teacher outcomes represent sound educational theory and practice.

# Chapter 4
# College and Community Connections

*Why should I become involved in organizations and service?*

*What kind of things should I do?*

*How do I get started?*

*What experiences build my reputation?*

*How do these experiences connect with my personal and professional goals?*

Prime candidates for teaching positions have developed interest areas and volunteer experiences that enhance their theoretical background and career interests. As you become involved in clubs, organizations and service activities, you broaden your knowledge and skills and develop a network of valuable relationships.

## Clubs and Organizations

Be sure to join honor societies and service and professional groups; there are many clubs and organizations at the college and in the community. Participation in those groups is time well spent. You acquire valuable knowledge and skills and you develop a network of peers and adult mentors.

It is worthwhile to join local, state and national professional organizations related to your field of study; there may be a chapter at the college or in the school district. For example, many teachers in the community belong to a local professional association that is affiliated with the state and/or national organization. Professional journals and other informative materials are typically included with membership. Attending local, state and national presentations and conferences helps you develop professional knowledge. Student memberships and fees are typically quite reasonable.

## Service Opportunities

Colleges often require service learning as a component of coursework and there is always a demand for volunteers in the community. Seek out these opportunities. Local newspapers publish information about food drives, blood drives, theater groups, art councils, summer concerts, soup kitchens, charitable groups, cultural groups, child care councils, museums, science centers, environmental groups and many more. While there are paid positions in these organizations, they could not operate without the help of volunteer time, energy and resources.

College experience in volunteer groups prepares you for engagement as a professional. When you enter teaching, participation in community groups is important for a number of reasons. As an educator in the community, you are a model and a leader. The community needs your contribution, and the groups depend on your participation. Involvement is also an opportunity to become acquainted with the members of the community and to become known as a person and a teacher.

While the community where you live or where you attend school may not be the community where you will be employed as a teacher, it is an excellent place to begin contributing your skills and resources, and it is a good place to develop your experience and reputation.

## Make a Good Match

Don't hesitate to join and participate in any group that needs you or interests you. You should also take the time to consider your own goals and interests, in order to find an organization that is a good fit. You may want to know more about the organizational aspects of providing services to children or you may want to develop your repertoire of skills and talents.

Joining a local organization like the Child Care Council allows you to work with adults who are involved with children in the age group you wish to teach. On the other hand, you may wish to work with a group that is more closely allied with a particular talent or interest: local theater groups always need members, for example. Some may sing, or dance or act; many others work behind the scenes on costumes, props, publicity and other important tasks. Each volunteer opportunity expands your horizons and your resume.

Take time to consider how the volunteer activities fit you as a person and a professional. In your work with these organizations, you may discover interests, skills or talents that you never recognized in yourself. All these experiences serve as an occasion to observe and participate in program planning and implementation, and to exert a leadership role within the organization. Participation builds a background of knowledge and expertise that enhances your professional development.

## Direct Experience with Children

Volunteer experiences and practical experiences associated with coursework often take students into the community and the schools to work with children. Involvement in classrooms, summer camps, sport programs, Big Brother-Big Sister organizations, literacy programs, etc. contributes to a candidate's professional expertise. You acquire a working knowledge of schools and other institutions that provide for the needs of children. You observe children's development and interactions. You practice skills communicating with and guiding children and you look closely at children's unique characteristics and life circumstances. Careful reflection on your experiences will help you identify and address questions, needs and concerns you may have about your role and about your prospective career.

## Employment

Most students are employed while attending college. Any job is an opportunity to build your skills and to network within the community. Your professional reputation is built upon a concern for excellence and a job well done. Volunteer sponsors, instructors and employers are aware of what you do and how you do it. Being known as prompt, dependable and hard working is worth its weight in gold. One administrator we know listed a factory job on his resume and included a reference from his employer. Many parents in the community that hired him were factory workers. The interview team believed that this candidate would understand and be responsive to the needs of children, parents and the community.

## Take an Active Approach to Building Your Reputation

Be mindful of your goal. You have much to contribute to these organizations; you also have many rewards to reap through participation. Find ways to help or take a leadership role; ask questions; build friendships. In addition to developing career skills and job-related knowledge, you demonstrate motivation, commitment and *people skills* that help make you a valued member of the group. You also build a relationship with professional and community people who can provide valuable mentoring, professional contacts and employment references.

## Document Your Experiences

Take care to collect information and artifacts related to your experiences. Most organizations have materials that describe their goals and function within the community. If it is permissible, take photographs as you participate.

Take time to organize the materials. Some individuals keep the materials from each different experience in a large envelope: on the envelope, they write the dates of their participation, events they supported or planned, and reflective comments about the things they did and learned.

Reflect upon the relevance of these experiences to your personal and professional goals. These materials will be a valuable resource as you build your portfolio, credential file and resume. This reflection helps you to prepare an application to graduate school or to prepare for an interview for a teaching position.

## Frequently Asked Questions

### How can I find volunteer opportunities?

Many colleges and universities have an Internship or volunteer office, where interested students can learn about opportunities to volunteer or engage in credit-bearing experiences. Local newspapers feature advertisements asking for volunteers.

### What is the best kind of volunteer experience for me?

Select a volunteer experience based on your interest and on its relationship to your goals or skills. Take a chance and try something new and different. You may discover a previously undiscovered interest area or talent.

### How many different volunteer experiences would be helpful to me as I prepare for my career?

While quality is more important than quantity, consistent experience throughout your college preparation program informs your career goals and develops your repertoire of skills. Familiarity with a range of ages is helpful. Some work with a community organization and/or an organization that provides services to children is helpful.

### Do interviewers find volunteer experiences worthwhile?

Volunteer experiences attest to a candidate's motivation and sense of service. Candidates who have worked with children of different ages in a variety of settings demonstrate a strong background for teaching.

# Chapter 5
# Certification

*What are the new requirements for certification in New York?*

*What steps must I take to be certified in my teaching field?*

In June 2000, the New York State Board of Regents adopted amendments to Part 80 of Commissioner's Regulations, establishing new requirements for the certification of classroom teachers. The new requirements for certification become effective February 2, 2004. Applicants for certification who apply and qualify for certification prior to that date must meet current requirements.

Candidates currently entering teacher education programs will in all likelihood apply for and/or qualify for certification after February 2004; they must meet the new requirements. The New York State Education Department web site provides the most up-to-date information on the situation, including a Comparison of Key Changes chart, which lists current regulations and the regulations that become effective in February 2004. Please refer to Chapter 9: *Resources* for the Web sites.

## New Certification Requirements

The following information, taken from the New York State Office of Teaching Initiatives, describes the new requirements, which go into effect in February 2004.

## Key Features of the New Certification Requirements

- New certificate titles and certificate forms

- New grade ranges, including early childhood (birth-grade 2), childhood (grades 1-6) and middle childhood (grades 5-9): Grades 7-12 remain the same.

- Completion of a coherent preparation program (tied to New York State student learning standards)

- Recognition of the equivalency of National Board Certification for initial certification

- Institution of the content specialty test (CST) requirement for the initial certificate

- Institution of a professional development requirement for valid professional certification

- Provision of a mechanism for career changers to enter the teaching field

- Elimination of the issuance of temporary licenses

To be employed in a public school in New York State, teachers must hold New York State Certification. In New York State, the term "teacher" refers to classroom teachers, administrative and supervisory personnel and pupil personnel service providers. At this time, the new certification requirements apply only to classroom teachers.

## Certification Areas and Levels

Certificates are issued by the Office of Teaching Initiatives and assure that the holder has met state requirements. Certificates may be obtained in a variety of areas related to teaching. The following list of Classroom Teaching Certificate Titles identifies only Common Branch Subjects (pre-K- grade 6) and subject areas (grades 5-12).

- **Early Childhood Education**    (birth – grade 2)

- **Childhood Education**    (grades 1- 6)

- **Middle Childhood Education**    (grades 5–9: Generalist)

- **English Language Arts**    (grades 5-9)

- **English Language Arts**    (grades 7-12)

- **Language other than English**    (specified) (grades 5-9)

- **Language other than English**    (specified) (grades 7-12)

- **Mathematics**    (grades 5-9)

- **Mathematics**    (grades 7-12)

- **Biology**    (grades 5-9)

- **Biology**    (grades 7-12)

- **Chemistry**    (grades 5-9)

- **Chemistry** (grades 7-12)

- **Earth Science** (grades 5-9)

- **Earth Science** (grades 7-12)

- **Physics** (grades 5-9)

- **Physics** (grades 7-12)

- **Social Studies** (grades 5-9)

- **Social Studies** (grades 7-12)

Certificates are issued in a great number of other areas, including but not limited to Special Subjects, Literacy, Students with Disabilities (various age/grade ranges), Literacy (birth-grade 6; grades 5-12) and English to Speakers of Other languages (all grades). In addition, Certification Extension Titles and Certificate Annotation Titles are available. Please consult The New York State Education Department Office of Teaching Initiatives or Web site for details about specific certificates. See Chapter 9 *Resources*.

## Requirements for the Initial (first) Certificate

It is possible to qualify for Initial Certification through interstate reciprocity. These arrangements pertain primarily to academic training in a teaching area; candidates are still obliged to complete other certification requirements. Check with the New York State Education Department: Office of Teaching for specific details.

Beginning in February 2004, the Commissioner of Education will issue an Initial Certificate, valid for up to 3 years upon evidence of completion of the following requirements:

- Completed baccalaureate degree in an approved teacher preparation program.

- Passing grade on three examinations:
- Liberal Arts and Science Test (LAST)
- Assessment of Teaching Skills-Written (ATS-W)
- Content Specialty Test (CST).

National Board certification qualifies a candidate for an Initial Certificate. National Board Certification is further discussed in Chapter 2 *Becoming a Teacher in New York State.*

## Application for Initial Certification

A completed Application for Certification must be submitted through appropriate channels at the college, or submitted to the New York State Office of Teaching Initiatives. Candidates may also apply through Regional Certification Offices located at the Regional Boards of Cooperative Educational Services (BOCES).

Application for Certification requires:

- Completion of State required workshops, including Child Abuse Recognition and Reporting (CARR) and Safe Schools Against Violence (SAVE).

- Completed fingerprinting/background check packet.

## CARR and SAVE Workshops

Many colleges require these State mandated workshops as part of the teacher preparation program. Candidates should check with the Education Department or Career Center for more information.

## Fingerprint-Supported Background Check

Effective July 1, 2001 applicants for certification and prospective employees of school districts, charter schools and Boards of Cooperative Educational Services (BOCES) must complete a fingerprint-supported criminal history background check.

Individuals who are applying for a permanent certificate and hold a valid provisional certificate, applied for prior to July 1, 2001 in the same title for which permanent certification is sought, are exempted from this requirement.

Information on the fingerprint-supported background check is usually available at Career Centers or Education Departments. Applicants may contact authorized law enforcement agencies to determine whether they offer fingerprinting services. For further information, see Chapter 9 *Resources*.

Please note that this information packet is sent to NY-SED and candidates do not receive a response unless additional information is required. There is a processing fee for the background check.

Once information on an individual is entered in the State Education Department database, there is no need to be fingerprinted again for future employment or additional certification applications as long as the individual has not been out of employment with a NYS school district, BOCES or charter school for a period exceeding 12 months.

Records will be destroyed for individuals who leave a position and do not secure employment at a public school, charter school or BOCES in New York State within 12 months. Individuals who seek employment after their fingerprints have been destroyed must be fingerprinted again.

For further information on the Fingerprint-Supported Background Check see Chapter 9 *Resources*.

## Validity of Initial Certificate

The Initial Certificate is valid for 3 years, with a possible one - year extension. Extensions may be granted upon completion of 24 semester hours of approved graduate study. The Initial Certificate may not be renewed. Issuance of the Initial Certificate may be delayed up to 2 years after program completion, if a candidate delays further study or employment (for example by joining the Peace Corps for two years). In some cases, the Initial Certificate may be reissued, upon completion of additional professional development.

## Requirements for Professional (Permanent) Certificate

Beginning in February 2004, the Commissioner of Education will issue a Professional (permanent) Certificate, upon evidence of completion of the following requirements.

- Satisfied requirements for the Initial Certificate.

- Completed master's degree from an approved teacher preparation program in a functionally related field. (Study in the master's program should be in a field closely related to the undergraduate teaching degree)

- Three years satisfactory teaching experience (either public or private school, or a combination of both), including one-year of mentored teaching experience

## Validity of Professional (permanent) Certificate

All teachers receiving a professional certificate after September 2000 must complete at least 175 hours of professional development every five years in order to maintain the certificate in good standing. School districts must provide professional development activities, directly related to identified needs, for teachers. The professional development should directly relate to student learning needs as identified in the School Report Card, state initiatives and the New York State standards and assessments.

## Transitional Certificates

Transitional Certificates will be issued to candidates in intensive, school-based teacher preparation programs and entry-level teacher in specific and career subjects. For more information on Transitional Certificates, see the web site
http://www.highered.nysed.gov/tcert/certificate/reqeffective.htm

## Assistance with the Application Process

Colleges and universities with registered teacher education programs provide information and assistance with application for Certification. Candidates should contact the Education Department, Registrar's Office or Dean's Office for details.

## Frequently Asked Questions

### May I student teach or graduate without taking the LAST, ATS-W and CST or the required workshops?

Individual colleges determine requirements for completing the LAST, ATS-W, CST and the State mandated workshops. Check department requirements for eligibility for student teaching.

### When should I take the Liberal Arts & Sciences Test (LAST)?

Although the tests may be taken at any time during undergraduate coursework, the majority of candidates take the LAST when they have completed most of their general education requirements, typically at the end of the second year or early in the third year.

### When should I take the Assessment of Teaching Skills-Written (ATS-W)?

The majority of candidates take the ATS-W after completing their pedagogy/methods courses, just before student teaching.

## When should I take the CST?

Most students take the CST during the senior year, while the coursework is still fresh in their minds. The CST is a graduation requirement for some teacher preparation programs. Please check with your department or Career Center for more information.

## How are test scores reported to the New York State Education Department?

Test scores are automatically reported by social security number to the Office of Teaching Initiatives after each test administration. Scores are retained there for five years, even if a candidate has not yet made formal application for a certificate.

## If I don't pass a test on the first try, how often may I retake it?

There is no restriction on the number of times a test may be taken.

## Can I retake just the parts of the test I don't do well on?

No. For each attempt, a candidate must take a test in its entirety, since passing standards are set on the total test rather than on sub area or partial scores. Candidates receive sub area scores on the score report, but these are provided only to help the candidate prepare effectively if the test must be taken again.

**If I already possess a certificate based upon NTE (National Teacher Examination) scores, must I take the NYSTEs to obtain an additional certificate in another title?**

Yes. All Candidates for a certificate must now take the NYSTCE tests.

**When should I expect to hear from the State Education Office about Initial Certification?**

Processing of applications for certification may take some time. It is best to allow several months for the New York State Education Department: Office of Teaching to process the application.

**I am applying for teaching positions. What do I tell a school district if I have not yet received my NYS certification or if I don't have my Initial Certificate in hand?**

You may apply for positions without having the Initial Certificate in hand. The cover letter may indicate that your certificate is pending. The Initial Certificate is a paper transaction from NY-SED. You may be hired pending your certification; note that all requirements must be met.

**How do I apply for certification in New York State if I have certification in another state?**

In most cases, candidates should apply directly to the New York State Education Department: Office of Teaching, which would send a packet of materials for completion. In some cases local school districts will help candidates through this process.

**What should I do if I want to apply for certification in another state?**

New York State has reciprocal agreements with many states. Applicants who have New York State certification and wish to apply for certification in another state should check with the New York State Education Department: Office of Teaching Initiatives for specific information on states having reciprocal agreements with New York. See chapter 9 *Resources* for the Web site. A Web site, which links to State Education Departments across the United States, is also provided.

# Chapter 6
# The Credential File and Marketing Plan

*What must I do to prepare for finding a position?*

*What materials must be ready for my application?*

*How do my experiences fit into my application materials?*

*How do my application materials present me to my best advantage?*

Before candidates reach the interview stage of the job search there are important preparatory activities to consider. Your academic experiences and volunteer experiences should be in place, supporting your performance. Your resume should be complete and up-to-date. You should have prepared a cover letter to accompany your application to school districts of your choice. You should have a collection of letters of reference in an established credential file (the file has been *opened*).

The application, cover letter and resume sent to a school district are extremely important. Consider the type of school and the district, for example a small rural school or a large urban school. It is appropriate for a candidate to note a particular interest or a relationship with the district in the cover letter. The language used in these materials displays your familiarity with the profession and your understanding of how it works. The use of educational terms and other "tools of the trade" are part of the marketing strategies used in applications, cover letters and resumes to highlight candidate qualifications for the job. Take care that every aspect of the materials is professional and maintains the dignity of the position.

Candidates communicate a great deal about their desirability through the way application materials are prepared.

## The Application

Some prospective employers require complete application materials, to be submitted along with the cover letter, resume, references and transcripts. Other employers request that the application be completed on the Web.

If the district requires completion of an application, candidates should plan responses carefully. It is important to read the form thoroughly before filling it out. Take care that every aspect, including penmanship or typing, spelling, grammar, word choice and statement of information is thoughtful, accurate and impeccably presented. Consider the stated needs of the district as well as your own interests and qualifications in crafting responses to questions.

## The Cover Letter

A cover letter should accompany the application and resume. The cover letter should always be addressed to a particular school district administrator, in most cases the Superintendent or the Assistant Superintendent for Personnel.

The letter should discuss how the candidate's skills match organizational needs and should emphasize areas parallel to the advertised job description. For example, if organizational skills come first in the job description, they should be addressed first in the letter.

## Addressing School District Characteristics

Each school district is unique and offers candidates a variety of experiences. Use web sites, community newspapers, school district publications, and other contacts to learn about the school and community. This information may be incorporated into the body of the letter.

## Essential Features of the Cover Letter

Cover letters are concise and immediately grab the reader's attention. Readers lose interest if they must wade through irrelevant information. The letter should state the purpose of the application, sell the reader on the need to hire the applicant and direct the reader to the resume.

The cover letter should be typed or word-processed in business format. The letter should be error free, easy-to-read and interesting. It should be elegantly designed, and presented on quality paper, which complements or matches the resume.

The letter should provide an address, telephone number and email address where an applicant may be reached. Take care that your email address has the professional quality and dignity required for the position. Similarly, any voice-mail message should be professional.

## Proofreading and Editing

Careful proofreading and editing is essential. Check for misspellings, omissions or improper grammar. Mistakes of this nature can cause immediate rejection of your application. It is helpful to have a trusted advisor proofread.

Reread for content, clarity and relevance to the job description. Is it an interesting letter that effectively profiles your qualifications, unique characteristics and personal style? For a checklist of typical cover letter components and a sample cover letter, see Chapter 9 *Resources*.

## The Resume

It is important to develop a resume early in the college career. Simply put, it is a summary of a candidate's experiences. It is a fairly straightforward document that is still creative and highlights your accomplishments. There is no one correct way to write a resume. The resume gives the reader an opportunity to quickly grasp a sense of your goals, experiences and unique qualities.

### Essential Resume Features

Resumes quickly profile a candidate's qualifications for the position. Resumes are typically read in 30 seconds or less, to determine the match between the organization's needs and candidates' skills and experiences. Typically, resumes for teaching position applications are one or two pages in length.

The resume format commands the reader's attention and presents the most important information first. The information relates your experiences to the career goal; irrelevant information such as gender, religion, race, etc. is omitted. This is not the time for modesty, but it is essential to be scrupulously honest and careful about style.

Resumes communicate a message about excellence, requiring an error free, professional presentation on quality paper.

An outstanding resume is the product of careful attention to preparation and organization. Models, guidance and direct assistance in preparing the resume can be found at most college and university Career Centers. For a checklist of typical resume components and a sample resume, see Chapter 9 *Resources*.

## The Credential File/Letters of Recommendation

Most college and university Career Centers maintain a credential service. The Credential Office maintains the file, which contains letters of recommendation (references). Upon written request, the Credential Office duplicates the letters, attaches an official campus cover page and mails the information to potential employers or graduate schools in a timely, professional manner. The credential file supports the cover letter, resume and application for a teaching position submitted by a candidate. Some colleges also provide transcripts from the Registrar's Office as part of this service. Candidates should check with the appropriate office at their institutions for more information. Official copies of transcripts can only be sent by the Registrar's Office.

### Establishing the Credential File

It is advisable to establish or *open* the file when you have begun the professional program at your college or university. The best time to obtain a reference is while currently interacting with the referring individual. As soon as a letter arrives in the Credential Office a file is automatically initiated; a candidate need not take any official steps at this point. *There is no cost to open a file (begin accumulating letters).*

A minimum of three letters is recommended. Candidates are encouraged to acquire more letters, which allows appropriate choices when the file is mailed.

## Activating the File

Many colleges and universities have a fee based credential file service; some provide the service free of cost. Typically, payment of a minimal fee for one calendar year or an established number of mailings, whichever comes first, will *activate* the file. Some institutions require payment by check or cash and do not accept payment by credit card. Candidates should check with the appropriate office at their institutions for more information.

Preparation and delivery of up to the established number of recommendations to one employer or graduate school is referred to as a *transmittal*. Typically, requests for transmittals must be in writing and must include the candidate's name, address, institutional identification number, telephone number and the address to which the file is to be sent. Requests are processed in order of receipt so it is advisable allow ample time to meet employer or graduate school requirements.

## References

Mentor teachers, school administrators, and college field experience supervisors typically provide letters of recommendation. If you have worked with children through volunteer or intern experiences, those supervisors are prime candidates for recommendations, as well. You may also wish to ask for references from college personnel, including instructors or faculty sponsors of clubs and organizations.

## Soliciting References

A good reference is developed through careful preparation. As you begin work with a sponsor or supervisor think about the statements you would like to see in the reference that individual writes for you. All would like be recognized for "excellence" and "integrity" and "professionalism." As you work with that person, what will you do to create that reputation?

When the time comes to request a reference, consider what you need to say and do. You should know ahead of time whether you will request a confidential or a non-confidential reference. When asking for a letter of reference, thoughtful individuals typically say something like "I'm developing my credential file, and wonder whether you would be willing to write a letter of recommendation for me." It is important to discuss the purpose of the letter with the writer and to ask what information is needed to aid in his/her support of your candidacy.

Be sure to provide the writer with a copy of the necessary form and a stamped envelope, addressed to the Credential Office, in which to send the letter. All letters should be professionally prepared, typed and attractive to the reader. Update the file regularly; new letters may be added to the file at any time.

## Confidential vs. Non-Confidential Letters of Reference

Pursuant to Public Law 93-380, references written on or after January 1, 1975 are open for inspection by the candidate unless the candidate has waived the right to access. If a letter includes the signed waiver of right of access, the letter becomes confidential and a candidate may not view the information that was provided; this decision is permanent. *Confidential letters may not be hand carried to potential employers: they must be mailed.* Non-confidential letters may be written on company letterhead or any other appropriate stationery. The decision to maintain a confidential or non-confidential file is the candidate's personal choice. Please consult the college or university Career Center staff for more information.

## Frequently Asked Questions

### What is the best length for a resume?

Typical education resumes are two pages in length, as they include student teaching, practicum experiences and a variety of volunteer, service learning and paid positions. District administrators often want to see the variety of experiences a candidate has to offer their school.

### What style is best for a resume?

Neutral colors are recommended: white, buff, gray, cream, etc. are good choices. Personal information and pictures of the candidate are not recommended. That does not mean that the resume must be boring. Creativity is greatly appreciated, including borders and headers, as long as the resume retains the dignity and professionality appropriate to the position.

## Should I list all my work experiences?

It is always helpful to list relevant experiences, for example where work with others, attention to detail, communication, team work, management and problem-solving ability apply to teaching.

## Can I develop a form letter for my cover letter?

No. A cover letter should always be addressed to a particular school district administrator. Each school district is unique and offers candidates a variety of experiences. Candidates should explore via the web, newspapers, school board minutes and personal contacts to learn about the school, and incorporate those qualities into the body of the letter.

## If I have a connection to the community, or a particular interest in working there, should I mention that in the cover letter?

Yes. Your interest in the community or your connection with the schools or a community member is pertinent information.

## Where can I find school district addresses and administrator names?

See *The Directory of Public School Administrators in New York State,* a booklet that lists all current school districts and schools, with names of schools, administrators, telephone numbers and addresses. BOCES administrators are included. See Chapter 9 *Resources* for the address.

# Chapter 7
# The Interview

*Who am I as a professional?*

*What do I want the interviewer to learn about me?*

*What must I do to prepare for this interview?*

*What helps me perform well in the interview?*

*How should I follow up, after the interview?*

Interviews offer candidates the opportunity to make a professional presentation of qualifications for a teaching position. That presentation is far more than the words uttered and the papers presented. School district representatives evaluate the candidate's appearance, qualifications, communication skills, enthusiasm and interest in children and teaching. Do you believe in first impressions? It has been said that the first four seconds of an interview can determine the outcome. Careful planning and research is a significant element in a successful interview.

## Envisioning the Interview

If an interview were as simple as a few answers, most of us would not become nervous. Questions represent an important factor in most of the decisions a school district makes about a candidate. The period before the interview is a critical time for reflection and preparation for questions.

Once the question is asked, a candidate is in control; exert that control to your best advantage. Districts are always looking for individuals who can enhance the entire school atmosphere. Ideally each person would bring unique attributes and experiences to broaden the total staff community. Come to the interview knowing and prepared to talk about what you will contribute to a school.

Most interview teams know the grade level and teaching qualifications needs of their district. They will often ask a candidate's preference for a particular grade or classroom type. Wise candidates articulate a preference while also affirming enthusiasm for a wider range of placements. Every position is a chance to learn and be an integral part of the school community.

Be prepared to discuss what you have to offer a district and make sure you know how to effectively communicate that message. Practice answers to questions before a mirror and in mock interviews. Remember to enjoy the interview and let that pleasure show.

Preparatory research relates directly to a candidate's performance. The best plan is specific to the match between the candidate and the district. The following suggestions will help you plan for the interview.

## Plan Ahead for All Aspects of the Interview

Use the Web to learn about the school district, the school calendar and other important information. Consult local media for community news, school board minutes, etc. Speak personally with local citizens about the school and community.

Be familiar with the particular issues and interests in the community.

Determine what it is about the school district that makes it appealing as a place to teach. Be prepared to tell the interviewers what you know about the district and why you would like to teach there. Relate your answers to the characteristics of the school and community.

Consider the match between school district needs and your own experiences. For instance, foreign language skills or tutoring experience would be helpful in a district with a significant ESL (English as a Second Language) population. Similarly, experience coaching or directing art or musical activities may make you an attractive candidate. All kinds of experiences are pertinent.

## Helpful Strategies for the Day of the Interview

Plan carefully for the day of the interview. Successful candidates know the names of the interviewers. They are familiar with the school district. They have reviewed possible interview questions and rehearsed answers.

Arriving 15-20 minutes early is wise. The interview may be at the school or at the district offices; the school secretary can usually provide directions. It is important to know the way to the interview site in advance; knowing the way allows a candidate to arrive on time, feeling assured and confident. Arriving late may mean the interview is over!

One administrator's advice is that a candidate should never be remembered for what was worn to the interview. A neat appearance testifies to a candidate's good judgment: clean, pressed clothing, polished shoes, understated hairstyle and make-up is recommended. This occasion requires business attire.

## Strategies to Present your Qualifications

Envision an interview as a stage play or a television performance with the candidate as star. Everything that occurs is significant, communicating part of the important message. What is seen, said and done has an impact on the outcome.

Take advantage of the opportunity to present yourself. Step forward with confidence and introduce yourself or respond immediately to a greeting. Make eye contact, and offer a smile and a firm handshake. Your demeanor should communicate that you look forward to the interview.

Follow the lead of the interview team, for the style of the interview. If the interviewers take a formal and serious approach, you should do the same. If they are casual and funny, you may be, as well. Be aware of the need to maintain professionality, however. There is a fine line between appropriate and inappropriate responses. It is always best to take a conservative approach. At the same time, do not abandon your own personality and style entirely.

Before you even speak, your attitude should say that you are eager to demonstrate your desirability as a candidate. Rehearse answers to sample questions before a mirror or with a colleague, so that you can answer completely and confidently.

## Responding to Questions in the Interview

Listen carefully to the whole question before you answer. Take needed time to consider your ideas and formulate your answer. It is acceptable to ask for a question to be repeated or clarified. Answer as completely as you can, and try to tailor the response to what you know of school district needs.

Recognize that the interviewers may ask a question that you cannot answer. In that case, say so. It is far better to say something like "I'm not familiar with that program. Can you tell me a bit more about it?" than to avoid or fake an answer. Interviewers don't expect that you will know everything; they do appreciate honesty and responsiveness.

Some interview questions can be intimidating. The interviewers may ask about a time you made a mistake or failed. Use the opportunity to describe an interaction that led you to reflect on your experience, and tell how you changed your approach and dealt with the situation successfully the next time. Your response to these kinds of questions tells the interview team a lot about how you meet challenges and how well you can work with administrators.

Be prepared to ask questions. The questions you ask the interviewers communicate a great deal about you as a candidate. This is the opportunity to learn about the school, State standards and curriculum, induction and professional development, etc. You may want to know more about particular community issues that affect the schools. The questions demonstrate your professional interests, knowledge of the field and the school district and also your ability to engage in professional dialogue.

Close the conversation gracefully. Beginnings and endings are the most important times in an interview. At the end of the interview, you will have an opportunity to highlight your accomplishments. Rehearse your summary so that you can effectively use this time to highlight the unique skills and qualities you would bring to the school system.

## Follow Up After the Interview

Many candidates make the mistake of thinking the interview ends when they depart from the building. To do so misses a vital opportunity to learn and to make a final impression upon the interview team. Make a few notes about the interview, in order to remember important details for a possible second interview and to assess your interview skills. Incorporate some of those details into a Thank You note. Call the school occasionally to see if you can supply any further information, if interviewers have indicated that this is acceptable.

## Typical Interview Questions

Interview teams tend to have favorite questions. The following examples will help you rehearse answers. Pay attention to the tone of your voice. Practice making eye contact and keeping your hands still. Smile! Your answer should respond to qualities as they relate to the needs of the district.

We have also included questions that candidates frequently ask, to help you prepare for the interview. Match questions to what you know of the district, and use the questions to highlight your unique potential in the district.

## Frequently Asked Interviewer Questions

Tell me about yourself.

What would you like me to remember about our interview?

Tell me about an aspect of student teaching that you found challenging.

What experience do you have with integrated curriculum?

What reading (math, science, etc.) program did you use in student teaching?

Describe a time when you had to act quickly to resolve an unexpected situation.

What experience do you have with mainstreaming or inclusion? What accommodations have you made to assist learners?

What do you consider important issues in education today?

How do you handle disruptive children? Give an example.

What discipline approach do you use? Why?

Was there ever a time when you made a mistake or didn't handle something well?

Why should I hire you?

## Frequently Asked Candidate Questions

Can you tell me a little about the students who attend the school?

What are some important issues in this community that impact the school?

What technology resources are available to classroom teachers?

What discipline approach/procedures are used as district policy?

Does the district utilize mentors, teacher aides or parent volunteers?

Are teachers encouraged to be active in extracurricular activities? Are they compensated?

What kind of mentoring and professional development support is offered to teachers?

What parent and community support does the school receive?

What issues or concerns are most significant to parents in this community?

# Chapter 8
# Employment Opportunities

*What is the best way to find the right job?*

*Who can help me in my search?*

*There are so many resources; which one is right for me?*

Careful planning and a strategic approach play a significant role in a successful job search. Career Centers typically post information on job openings and recruitment events. A careful search of media from a desired locale can also pinpoint these opportunities. Wise candidates network effectively and talk with prospective employers as often as possible.

## Networking

If you ask how someone got a job, the response is frequently "networking" or "I just heard about it." Candidates often wonder, "What is *networking* and how is it done?"

- A *network* can be a group of friends or acquaintances.

- A *network* can be a professional organization.

- A *network* can be your professors and campus staff.

- A *network* can be your relatives and neighbors.

- A *network* is any group with a common interest or link to a particular field, organization or type of position.

*Networks* provide a link to a project, activity or professional contact.

*Networks* are not placement: networks don't "give" a job to a candidate. They will not guarantee an interview or even guarantee consideration. *Networks* help but they do not do the job search for the candidate.

*Networks* give a slight edge, which can lift a resume and cover letter out of the pile and enhance an application.

Employers report receiving as many as 500 resumes for a single position. *Networking* allows someone to say, "I understand that Mary Smith applied for that position. I have worked with her and I am certain that she will be a strong candidate." Employers tell of needing specific skills, and not knowing how to find them. *Networking* allows a colleague to say, "John Doe can do that. Would you like me to ask him to call you?"

*Networks* are developed at association meetings, conferences, alumni meetings, in conversation with professors, at dinner with friends, and so on. *Networks* are maintained by keeping in touch with those associates, by telling them what you are doing and by giving them information and assistance on a regular basis.

*Networks* are fostered by collecting business cards, keeping records, maintaining communication and demonstrating sincerity. Networking doesn't work unless you give as well as get. You must always say thank you and follow through on suggestions or introductions, as well as reciprocate!

Most *networking* successes come from associates seen as little as once a year. To build such a network requires regular letter writing, phone calls and other non-personal contacts.

College students have a special *network:* the Alumni Association. Alumni live all over the country and are employed in every possible line of work. Make friends with alumni in your area, attend alumni events and activities, and be a friend to those alumni who seek you out.

When you have begun your professional career and have joined the ranks of the alumni, take an active role supporting the Alumni Association and *networking* with the new group of candidates who seek your help.

## Recruitment Events and Employment Fairs

For many, the thought of going to an educational employment fair can be both exciting and intimidating. Some candidates view a job fair as the quickest way to secure a position with a school district. Others view it as a way to examine options and openings in many school districts, as well as to network and gather information. An employment fair is a wonderful opportunity for every candidate to learn about the job market and to practice skills for the job search.

As you prepare for a recruitment event, it is important to understand your professional goals and strengths and be prepared to discuss them. Plan carefully for the event.

Interview attire is neat, business oriented and understated. Personal grooming should be impeccable.

Careful preparation is vital. At a job fair, candidates have a very brief chance to present their qualifications and make an impression on an interviewer.

Consider the types of schools and locations you prefer. Know where you are willing to go and prepare to discuss your preferences. Know what districts will attend; you can even call to ask if you can make an appointment for an interview at the upcoming fair. Your proactive approach will be appreciated.

Gather information on target school districts and become familiar with the information. Use the Web, local newspapers, personal contacts, etc. Almost all districts have web sites and interviewers expect candidates to know something about them.

Practice and rehearse your presentation and responses. Participate in many practice interviews. Candidates must impress a district administrator very quickly; typical job fair interviews last 15 to 30 minutes.

Make copies of your resume and transcripts to hand out.

Prioritize first and second choice schools, etc. in order to make the best use of your time and opportunities at the fair.

## At the Recruitment Fair

Once again, prioritize your approach. Confirm that the target district is seeking someone in your certification area. Have copies of your resume and transcripts ready. Make appointments and *keep* them.

When you meet with an interviewer, present yourself
effectively. Take an active role; do not simply wait for
questions. Demonstrate why you are a desirable candidate:
articulate your message briefly and powerfully, with a smile.
End gracefully and thank the interviewer for taking time to talk
with you.

Be sure to obtain business cards or other material from target
districts. Ask if you may follow up in a few weeks.

**After the Interview**

Take time to make a few notes about the interview and the
school and district. Send a Thank You note to the interviewer
within a few days; it need not be typed, but should be
impeccably presented. Reiterate your qualifications,
highlighting skills and information you want the interviewer to
remember. Contact the school within a two-week period to ask
if any additional information on your candidacy is needed.

## Vacancies on the Web

As more school districts develop web sites, they are using the
Web to post vacancies. Most college Career Centers have some
sort of Web based vacancy list. The New York State Education
Department Office of Teaching Initiatives provides links to job
banks on its Web site. See Chapter 9: *Resources* for more
information.

## Virtual Job Fairs

A Virtual Job Fair (VJF) is an opportunity for candidates to use the Internet to explore job openings and post their resumes 24 hours a day, 7 days a week. A VJF may offer an application process and in some cases start the interview process.

A college or university Career Center, a consortium (group of colleges) or a business that specializes in educational virtual job fairs typically coordinates a VJF. For more information, check with your college or university Career Center.

As with any other interview, plan carefully before entering information and responses. Spelling and grammar should be correct; language should be clear and professional. In every way, you should effectively demonstrate your desirable qualifications for a position.

## Frequently Asked Questions

### When I want to network, how do I go about it?

Whether speaking with strangers or acquaintances, say something like "I'm beginning a job search for a teaching position. Do you know of information or contacts that might be helpful?"

### Where can I find more information about Employment Fairs and Virtual Job Fairs?

Check with the Career Center at your college or university. See Chapter 9 *Resources* for more information.

# Chapter 9
# Resources

The following information on offices, Web sites and publications can help you find the answer to a question or learn more about an area of interest. We encourage you to visit the Career Center at your college or university, and to consult the Web sites often. Information develops and changes rapidly.

Checklists and samples of application cover letters and resumes are included at the end of the chapter.

## Certification and Employment Requirements

For more information on certification, please check the New York State Education Department, Office of Teaching Initiatives Web site.
http://www.highered.nysed.gov/tcert

You may also contact the office by mail or telephone:

> New York State Education Department
> Office of Teaching Initiatives
> Albany, NY  12234

Telephone  (518) 474-3901
9:00-11:30 a.m., 1:30-4:30 p.m. eastern time
Monday-Tuesday and Thursday-Friday for Office of Teaching Initiatives representative assistance
For automated information, call any time.
Relay center telephone number for the deaf within New York State:  (800) 421-1220 (TTY)

## Comparing Old and New Certification Requirements in New York State

For more information about changes in certification requirements, see the New York State Education Department of Teaching Initiatives Comparison of Key Changes in Regulations for Certification. Follow the links found at http://www.highered.nysed.gov

## New York State Teacher Certification Examinations (LAST; ATS-W; CST)

Descriptions of the required tests, registration forms and dates/location of examinations are listed in the New York State Teacher Certification Examinations Registration Bulletin (NYSTCE). The test booklet is available at Career Centers, Education Department Offices or Dean's Offices at colleges. Please contact the NYSTCE web site for details and on-line registration at http://www.nystce.nesinc.com. Dates and locations are listed in the test application booklet.

For questions regarding test registration, administration procedures, and admission or score reports, contact:

> NYSTCE
> National Evaluation Systems, Inc.
> P.O. BOX 660
> Amherst, MA 01004-9008

Telephone: (413) 256-2882
Telephone number for the deaf: (413) 256-8032 (TTY)

To obtain recorded NYSTCE Program information, you may call National Evaluation Systems (413) 256-2882 or (800) 309-5225, 24 hours a day, 7 days a week, from a touch-tone telephone to receive recorded information regarding:

- test dates, registration deadlines, test fees, types of payment accepted, and score reporting mailing dates
- internet registration
- how to obtain a registration bulletin or preparation guide
- how to add to, change, or withdraw your registration

- score reports
- how to obtain an additional score report
- how to have a test re-scored
- how to request alternative testing arrangements

To speak with a Customer Service Representative at National Evaluation Systems, call (413) 256-2882, 9:00 a.m. - 5:00 p.m. eastern time, Monday-Friday, excluding holidays. To speak to a customer service representative, follow the instructions provided.

## Additional Information on Fingerprint Supported Criminal History Background Check

In addition to the information included in the fingerprinting packet, more information is available from the Office of School Personnel Review and Accountability (OSPRA) at (518) 473-2998 or OSPRA@mail.nysed.gov. If an individual's information remains in the State Education Department database, there is no need to be fingerprinted again for future employment or additional certification applications.

## Code of Ethics for Educators: New York State Standards and Practices Board

Inquiries about the proposed Code of Ethics for Educators may be directed to the State Professional Standards and Practices Board for Teaching. You may write, telephone or E-mail:

Nancy Taylor Baumes
Secretary, State Professional Standards and Practices
Board for Teaching
New York State Education Department
Office of Teaching, Room 5N EB
Albany, New York 12234

Fax: (518) 473-0271
E-mail: nbaumes@mail.nysed.gov

## Job Search Resources

**New York State Clearinghouse for Teacher Recruitment**
Applications for teacher certification invite candidates to indicate a desire to have their name, address and certificate title(s) provided to the Statewide Clearinghouse for Teacher Recruitment and to local school districts. The names of applicant who respond in the affirmative and whose certification eligibility is subsequently established will be posted on the electronic Clearinghouse system. The information will remain on the system for eight months from the date it was entered. A name may be reactivated or added by a certificate holder by payment of a fee and application for a duplicate certificate. Follow the links at http://www.nysed.gov

### Incentive Programs

New York State is proposing and enacting a number of programs to attract and prepare minority candidates and candidates for high need areas.

### Teacher Incentive Program

A legislative proposal to support a competitive Teacher Incentive Program to attract or prepare well-qualified, certified teachers in certification areas and schools with shortages has been developed.

- Qualified undergraduates will be awarded $4,000 scholarships annually for a maximum of four years with the obligation to teach in an eligible school one year for each annual award.

- Qualified graduate students will be awarded a $10,000 scholarship for one year with an obligation to teach three years in an eligible school.

- Qualified certified applicants will receive a $10,000 bonus with the obligation to teach three years in a high-need eligible school. Permanent or professional Certification and strong recommendations from the most recent employing school and other screening requirements would apply.

Please follow the links at www.nysed.gov for updated information.

**Teachers of Tomorrow Program**

An amendment to Education Law, chapter 62 of the Laws of 2000 provides funds to assist school districts in the recruitment, retention and certification activities necessary to increase the supply of teachers in districts experiencing a teacher shortage, especially those in low-performing schools. Interested individual teachers may contact a local district to determine if that district is participating and then may apply through the local district. For further information see www.highered.nysed.gov/kiap/TRDE/tot/section1.htm.

**Links to Job Banks**
The New York State Office of Teaching provides links to Job Banks. Please check the site for updated information. Here are some useful links.

- TEACHNY Listings in the New York City Public Schools www.teachny.com

- New York City Board of Education www.nycenet.edu

- The Lower Hudson Valley On-line Application System for Educators serves over 60 school districts in Westchester, Putnam, Rockland and Orange counties www.pnwboces.org/teacherapplication

- NYEDJOBS Search this site for all listings. www.nyedjobs.org

- Dutchess County BOCES Search this site for job listings in Dutchess County and Ulster County www.dcboces.org

- NY EDUCATION JOBS Search this site for job listings statewide. www.nyeducationjobs.com

- TROOPS TO TEACHERS Access to this job site is open to all prospective teachers and all registered school districts www.jobs2teach.doded.mil

## Other Internet Sites

### Online Recruiting Services
America's Job Bank  http://www.ajb.dni.us/
The Monster Board http://www.monster.com/
Interactive Employment http://www.espan.com/
Career Mosaic http://www.careermosaic.ocm/cm/
Job Web http://www.jobweb.com/
Job Bank USA http://www.jobbankusa.com/
Yahoo's Employment Information http://www.yahoo.com
Teachers to Teachers http://www.Teachers-Teachers.com
American Association for Employment in Education www.aaee.org

### No-Cost Resume Posting Sites
Career Mosaic http://www.careermosiac.com/cm/
The Monster Board http://www.monster.com

## *Helpful Printed Material*

### *Directory of Public School Administrators in New York State*
To obtain a copy of this document, write to
> The University of the State of New York,
> The State Education Department,
> Information, Reporting and Technology Services
> Albany, NY 12234 or www.nysed.gov

### *101 Grade A Resumes for Teachers, 2nd Edition*
Rebecca Anthony and Gerald Roe. 1998, Barron's Educational Series, Inc.
ISBN 0-7641-0129-3

### *Job Search Handbook for Educators*
This is a great reference book for all stages of a job search including job
Web sites and all state certification Web sites.
American Association for Employment in Education, Inc.
3040 Riverside Drive, Suite 125
Columbus, OH  43221-2550
Telephone 614-485-1111
www.aaee.org

## Typical Cover Letter Components

- **Name, mailing address, telephone number, and email address** of applicant

- **Correct date**

- **Correctly spelled name of reader, title of organization and complete address**

- **Salutation**  Dear Mr. or Ms. Specific Name

- **Opening paragraph** Arouse the reviewer's interest. State why you are writing and why you are interested in this organization. It is helpful to state the source of your information (drop a name, mention a personal connection to the organization, location of advertisement, etc).

- **Body paragraph** Present skills and achievements that meet school/district needs. Briefly state accomplishments. Discuss personal attributes and unique qualifications, highlighting how you can assist the organization. Personalize and target the descriptions to the school or school district.  Four or five items should be sufficient.

- **Body paragraph** Cite information that refers the reader to the resume for a more detailed description of experience and background. Note that other items may be included with the letter such as the completed application, writing samples, etc. You may refer to them here.

- **Closing paragraph:** State future action that is desired. If you wish to call the reader in two weeks to arrange a convenient time to interview, the closing should say so. Be sure to call!  Tell how you can be reached for an interview. Be sure you are available! State that you will be happy to supply additional materials, if they are needed.  Be sure to say thank you.
- **Closing**
- Sincerely,

- (Your signature)
- (Your name typed)

# Sample Cover Letter

221 College Street
Any City, State 12345
March 28, 2003

Mary Jones Ph.D., Superintendent
Anyplace School District
City, State 12347

Dear Dr. Jones:

Please consider me as an applicant for the high school history position currently being advertised by Anyplace School District. I recently learned of your teaching opening from the Career Services Office at the State University of New York, Cortland College where I will earn my bachelor's degree in May of this year with a major in history and a minor in English.

As the enclosed resume indicates, I am completing a full semester internship at City High School working with a diverse student population in grades seven through twelve. In addition to my classroom experiences teaching American History, World History from 1700, Twentieth Century American Authors, and ninth grade Basic English, I volunteer to work individually and in small groups with the school's newspaper staff. I am particularly interested in your advertised opening because of the specific teaching responsibilities and the opportunity to advise the student magazine and work with other student publications. In addition to my education in the U.S., I was fortunate to do a study abroad in Scotland where I studied European History from a UK perspective.

As your advertisement requires, I have completed the school district's application on the World Wide Web and am currently arranging for the Registrar's Office to submit my transcripts to you. My letters of recommendation are being sent from the Career Services Office. I would welcome the opportunity to interview with your selection team and I look forward to hearing from you in the near future.

Sincerely,

Louie Larson
Enclosure

## Typical Resume Components

- **Name, address, telephone number, and email address** of applicant

- **Objective** The objective describes the position/field in which the candidate wants to work.

- **Education** List degrees, achievements, GPA, honors, awards, scholarships, languages, overseas academic experience, etc.

- **Teaching Experience** (Includes student teaching and practicum)

- **Employment Experience** List job titles and employing organization, dates, and notable achievements. Experience includes paid and unpaid work, part-time and full time work, internships and volunteer positions. Organize experiences in support of the employment goal(s), in order of importance.

- **Activities** A description of participation in campus and community activities demonstrates qualities of leadership, teamwork, organization, and interpersonal relations.

- **Interests** A description of interests profiles skills and interests that are relevant but may not fit in another category.

- **Other** This area notes information such as *Willing to Relocate, References on Request*, etc.

## Areas to Consider for the Resume

- Study Abroad

- Honors/Scholarships

- Skills relevant to teaching or school needs

- Certifications or licenses

- Awards/Achievements

# Sample Resume

---

**NAME**_____
123 College Ave.  University, NY  00011                    Telephone 123-45-6789

**CAREER OBJECTIVE**
To secure an Elementary Education teaching position that will challenge my talents and expertise in the teaching field, with the opportunity to direct children's theater.

**EDUCATION**
Bachelor of Science in **Elementary Education**, Concentration in **Psychology for the Exceptional Child** State University of New York College at Cortland, Cortland, NY May 2002 Cumulative G.P.A.: 3.58/4.0; Major G.P.A.: 3.95/4.0

**TEACHING EXPERIENCE**

**Student Teacher:** Ithaca Public School District, Ithaca, NY (Fall 2001)
*Worked cooperatively with master teacher in self-contained grade 4 class with 26 students.
* Used NYS Learning Standards to develop lessons in all curricular areas.
*Developed Social Studies unit on Indian Nations of North America, focused on housing. Cooperative groups created a model of a specific Indian Nation home for culminating project.
*Prepared bulletin boards and displays of student work inside and outside of the classroom.
*Observed and modeled master teacher's assertive approach to teaching social skills.
*Attended and participated in parent/teacher conferences, in order to develop rapport with parents.

**Student Teacher:** Syracuse City School District, Syracuse, NY (Fall 2001)
*Worked with master teacher and teacher aides in an inclusion classroom with 13 Pre-K students.
*Developed a strong working relationship with the classroom support staff, including two paraprofessionals, a Speech Therapist, Social Worker, Physical Therapist, Occupational Therapist and Family Worker.
*Created and implemented lessons based on NYS Learning Standards with modifications for students with special needs. Planned and taught unit on Winter with activities focused upon sharing skills and sight word identification.
*Participated in parent/teacher conferences, student IEP meetings, staff meetings and support staff meetings.

**Practicum:** Binghamton City School District, Binghamton, NY (Spring 2000)
*Completed 75 hours of observation/participation in a grade 3 classroom.
*Assisted mentor teacher with lessons and classroom activities focused on cooperation and Material Science.

**Safety Town Instructor:** Town of Amherst, Buffalo, NY (June 1999-Aug.1999)
*Oversaw experiences of 50 children ages 4-5 and 15 teenage volunteer workers in a 2-week Safety program.
*Worked closely with another instructor and volunteers during the program.
*Developed rapport with parents by creating newsletters and talking with them daily.

## WORK EXPERIENCE

**Substitute Teacher,** Sachem Central School District, Holbrook, NY (Jan. 2001-Present)
*Substitute teaching for a variety of grade levels in the Sachem district during college breaks.

**College Intern,** Blue Cross and Blue Shield, Excellus Health Plan Inc. Rochester, NY (June 2001-Aug. 2001)
*Created lesson plans for training adult learners in the Sales and Marketing Department.
*Utilized computer skills to create and edit training material.

**Resident Assistant,** University at Stony Brook, Stony Brook, NY (Jan. 2000-May 2001)
*In charge of a floor of 60 residents, establishing relationships in the dormitory, enforcing rules and creating and presenting hall programs related to safety, social and/or educational needs.
*Created educational bulletin boards on drug/alcohol safety, academic skills and support, career opportunities, etc.

**Orientation Assistant,** New York University, New York, NY (June 2000-Aug. 2000)
*Worked closely with parents of incoming first-year students and answered questions about the college and college programs.
*Conducted campus tours focusing on the different services NYU offers to students and parents.

## VOLUNTEER EXPERIENCE
Pinebrook Elementary School, Kingston Central Schools, Kingston, NY (Summer 2000)
*Volunteered in a Kindergarten classroom for a total of 35 hours during college break.
*Assisted the teacher. Interacted with the children and provided classroom support.

## COMPUTER SKILLS

Windows; Microsoft Word; Excel; Power Point; Internet use.

## REFERENCES

Written references available upon request from College of St. Rose Credential Office 123-456-7890

## Resume Checklist

- The resume is well designed, error free, professional in appearance.

- The focus of the resume is clear to the reader.

- The format is supportive of a 30 second skimming.

- Categories and supporting material are organized by pertinence to the desired position.

- Significant accomplishments are presented.

- The text has been edited to eliminate unnecessary words.

- Several proofreaders have reviewed/critiqued the resume.